SO YOU WANT TO BE AN ENGINEER

D1073026

A DEFINITIVE GUIDE TO THE CHALLENGES AND OPPORTUNITIES OF ENGINEERING

DAN H. HEFLIN, JR., P.E.

outskirts press

So You Want to Be an Engineer
A Definitive Guide to the Challenges and Opportunities of Engineering
All Rights Reserved.
Copyright © 2020 Dan H. Heflin, JR., PE
v2.0

The opinions expressed in this manuscript are solely the opinions of the author and do not represent the opinions or thoughts of the publisher. The author has represented and warranted full ownership and/or legal right to publish all the materials in this book.

This book may not be reproduced, transmitted, or stored in whole or in part by any means, including graphic, electronic, or mechanical without the express written consent of the publisher except in the case of brief quotations embodied in critical articles and reviews.

Outskirts Press, Inc.
http://www.outskirtspress.com

ISBN: 978-1-9772-3021-8

Cover Photo © 2020 www.gettyimages.com. All rights reserved - used with permission.

Outskirts Press and the "OP" logo are trademarks belonging to Outskirts Press, Inc.

PRINTED IN THE UNITED STATES OF AMERICA

Table of Contents

Disclaimer

This work is intended as a personal insight into the motivations for, and pursuit of, an engineering degree; and as an encouragement to anyone considering such an ambition. It is not offered as legal or financial advice nor for college selection, but solely presents and discusses the observations and understandings that accrued to the author during his college education; a long career comprising service in the US Army Corps of Engineers; a major corporate employee; and as a Registered Professional Engineer in private practice. Anyone intent on pursuing enrollment in engineering should seek specific college entry requirements directly from the colleges of interest. Financial and legal advice should be sought from appropriate licensed professionals

Dedication

This book is dedicated to the memory of those who made my engineering career possible and who encouraged me to stay the course in turbulent times. At the head of the list of my enablers are, of course, my devoted parents, Dan Hugh Heflin, Sr., and Anne Taylor Heflin and my Godmother, Ethel Wilburn. I am also deeply indebted to my Norfolk, Virginia's Maury High School Teacher, Champe C. Douthat, who guided me to undertake all of the math courses then offered at Maury High. Finally, to my wife and muse, Trish, my sincere appreciation for her encouragement and support in this project

Introduction

Since you are reading this book I assume you have a serious interest in engineering as your future college and business career. You probably are seeking some "inside" information on just what that would involve and what it will take to earn that qualification.

My objective in this book is to introduce anyone considering Engineering as a major in college and a subsequent career, to some of the realities of the educational process and the ensuing career opportunities and experiences. With the present emphasis on Science, Technology, Engineering, and Mathematics [STEM], high schoolers and recent graduates are being pressed to consider a career in STEM. This focus derives from a primary objective to dilute the heavy concentration of males in the sciences by convincing females, who have not traditionally chosen STEM based careers, to consider STEM. In doing so, the advocates' focus has been on the valuable, exciting and glamourous accomplishments of STEM practitioners. My goal is to present a realistic introduction to the whole spectrum of Engineering, and to allay shallow impressions in favor of a realistic look at the "real deal". Author Note: the use of "College" throughout refers to both Colleges and Universities.

If you are a recent or soon-to-be high school graduate, or an earlier grad presently working in what you consider to be an unsatisfying job and are considering improving your future through an engineering education, you apparently believe that Engineering may be your ticket to better career choices. The highly publicized social, professional and societal endorsement of STEM (Science, Technical, Engineering and Mathematics), especially for young ladies, paints a strong argument for such a choice. That has focused attention to the many aspects of engineering, citing excellent earnings potential, market demand for engineers, and the dramatic attraction of increasingly technical systems, machines, devices, products and robotics.

Many young folks are encouraged to consider an engineering career by their relatives who may be engineers, or by friends who work with or around engineers. Many have been encouraged by school advisors or by enthusiastic teachers. Others have developed interest through their own curiosity and desire to know and understand the logic behind machines and devices. Whatever the stimulus that brings you to giving serious consideration of an engineering education, you are entitled to a frank and open discussion of just what engineering actually is. It is a very wide-ranging field of study and experiences that prepare one for a challenging career that should also be satisfying, exciting, and rewarding... or it can be a crashing bore! Your experience will depend entirely upon your innate technical and academic aptitude and the intensity of your commitment to an engineering education and pursuit of career. In your choice, you will be challenged by a rigorous exploration and develop a comprehension of the involved sciences, changing your curiosities into understanding. Please consider this book to be a direct personal conversation between the two of us. In it, I will attempt to anticipate your questions and provide answers that I have developed through my personal and observed experiences. This is not intended to be a lecture, but rather a response to questions that I asked or should have asked, had I been experienced enough to recognize the issues. Hopefully, these pages will provide the information you will need to decide whether you really want to invest your time, energies, and money to become an engineer.

In this book we shall examine the three phases of accomplishing your goal of an engineering career.

- Part 1, Preparing For College
- Part 2, At College
- Part 3. Post-college Careers

I will attempt to familiarize you with what the study of engineering comprises and with what is involved and required in your college experiences for you to earn an Engineering Degree and make engineering your career:

If you are still interested in this challenge....carry on!

Part One
Preparing for College

CHAPTER 1

Engineering – My Observations

WHO AM I to presume to introduce you to Engineering? I am not a high school teacher, nor a professor in a college or university, nor a corporate trainer. I am simply the voice of one experienced practitioner; a retired certified Professional Engineer, with 65 years of experiences. Over that span of years, I have participated in a wide variety of projects ranging from parametric design studies, to detailed design, to program management. In those capacities, I have gained considerable experience with absorbing on-the-job training from experienced veterans, and talented tradesmen. I have learned that experience is the most powerful teacher one can employ. I have also learned to respect the practical experiences of tradesmen and their opinions and guidance. Later in my career, I joined another engineer in forming a private consulting practice in support of a wide range of projects being considered or launched. That led to my being retained as an expert witness for law firms across the nation that were engaged in marine and product litigation.

I was educated in Norfolk Virginia Public schools, graduating high school in 1949. I then enrolled at Virginia Polytechnic Institute in Mechanical Engineering. Like most high-schoolers, I had only a vague understanding of what that path would actually incur. I did have the benefit of a pre-graduation aptitude test that suggested my suitability for further technical education, but that actually only confirmed my ability to comprehend relatively complex concepts and associated mathematics. It did not elaborate on scope or content. My father was a pharmacist and my mother was a former bookkeeper. Neither of them had a background of any friends or relatives having had any engineering experience, so I depended on my school advisors and my personal inclinations.

From early childhood, I was drawn to mechanical toys and devices, and fascinated by them. I experimented with them by taking them apart and reassembling them. My favorite toys were anything that moved, performed a function or made noise. I soon developed a fascination with two magazines; "Mechanics Illustrated" and "Science Illustrated". With World War Two raging on, I was in a fertile location for naval and military equipment since Norfolk was a typical Navy Town with a concentration of shipyards and naval operations. Norfolk was and is a major Naval Fleet location, and a major USAF airbase is located just a few miles away. Military and naval equipment was quite visible and presented frequent sightings of ships and planes. Building and flying model planes became an obsession.

Both of my parents and my godmother, were insisting that I "go to college" after high school. The war ended well before I reached an age when military service would have been mandated. The impact of the war, however, did lead me to a college that afforded a path to commissioned military status; hence, Virginia Polytechnic Institute (VPI). VPI was and remains the leading engineering college in Virginia, and, as a Land-Grant college, was then, essentially a full time male Reserve Officer Training Corps (ROTC) college. In fact, every male applicant who was not a veteran and was physically fit, was required to be in the Corps of Cadets for the first two years after which it was elective. A perfect fit for my totally naïve selection of academic and military training!

I enrolled in Mechanical Engineering and the full-time Corps of

Cadets at VPI. Thus began an incredible journey into the unknown. Suddenly, all that was once a teenager's ideal and relatively care-free existence became a rigidly structured, two-sided daily grind. The dual shock of demanding academic requirements and equally demanding cadet compliance made each day and night a challenge. The academic demands made high school requirements pale into comparative insignificance. To my chagrin I was a mediocre student! I had found high school to be deceptively easy. The markedly increased demands of college were a shock. Class lectures and exercises were like drinking from a fire hose and demanded committing to unfamiliar dedication to study and concentration. Being in the Cadet Corps was a blessing in that it mandated restricted study time and complete adherence to schedules. Every waking hour was regulated, with prompt consequences for non-compliance. I found the demands to be swim or sink! In retrospect, I am forever grateful for the commitment it demanded and guaranteed.

As I progressed in ME, I came to realize that the intensely theoretical focus of the final year of ME was not likely to lead to the future I wanted. I recognized that my interest was more focused on applying the sciences of engineering to actual applications in design and product manufacturing. That convinced me (and a group of other similarly-minded men) to investigate other engineering degree programs. Several of us found our desired goal in the College of Industrial Engineering, now widely known as "Industrial and Systems Engineering". Because of the differing course requirements, transferring to that school involved accepting a commitment to a significant overload of credit hours for my entire senior year, including a full summer schedule. A further complication was my contractual ROTC commitment to two years of active military duty upon completion of four years in the Corps of Cadets and an extensive summer training camp at Fort Belvoir. I was subsequently commissioned a Second Lieutenant in the U.S. Army, Corps of Engineers, and served the required two years of active duty, but that is another story!

My first position after military service and my return to VPI for graduation was with E. I. DuPont's Chambers Works in New Jersey. It was in the Methods & Standards Department and, true to my IE degree, it was an entry level position in evaluating and measuring worker performance and rating. I quickly determined that, flattered as I was by DuPont's offer of employment, I soon realized that Methods and Standards was not my cup of tea. I hungered for system and machinery design work. I was interviewed by many companies prior to graduation, and one that struck a chord with me was Newport News Shipbuilding. They had even made a post-interview employment offer that I had declined in favor of the flattering DuPont offer. After discussions with my management at DuPont, I recognized that my future path there was not in the areas I desired, I resigned, swallowed my pride, and sought a fresh offer from NNS. They reinstated their original offer and I quickly accepted assignment to the Machinery Design Department as a Junior Designer. There, I had to learn a whole new business from the keel up, taught by an incredible group of skilled Designers and Supervisors that guided my experiences through on-job-training. Thus began my 36 year career that provided progressive positions from novice Designer into senior management as Director of Engineering Services. In my career at NNS, I enjoyed participating in numerous programs involving Tankers, Freighters, Passenger Liners, Aircraft Carriers, and Submarines. I was also challenged by assignments to the design and development of several methods and special devices that were urgently needed to resolve production and inspection holdups with certain critical components. During that employment, I was admitted to and passed the Virginia State examination for certification as a Registered Professional Engineer (RPE). In 1992, I retired from NNS after 36 very enjoyable years.

Following my retirement from NNS, I joined with another shipyard retiree to form a consulting practice to provide technical services to a wide variety of clients in the marine world. That 28 year second career provided many challenging and enjoyable opportunities from ship and yacht construction management to expert witness services. We assisted many nation-wide law firms engaged in numerous law suits involving plaintiffs claims for damages from exposure to a host of asbestos-containing products that were used in building, repairing or operating ships.

Suffice it to say that I have thoroughly enjoyed my career and heartedly recommend such a career to anyone with similar motivation and interest. It is a demanding challenge but one rich in rewards of satisfaction and accomplishment.

CHAPTER 2

What Is Engineering?

Definitions of Engineering:

* According to Webster's Encyclopedic Unabridged Dictionary Of The English Language 1989: 1. "The art or science of making practical application of the knowledge of pure sciences, as physics, chemistry, biology, etc.; 2. The action, work or profession of the engineer; 3. Skillful or artful contrivance."
* According to Webster's Seventh New Collegiate Dictionary 1970: 1. The art of managing engines; 2. A science by which the properties of matter and the sources of energy in nature are made useful to man."

From the definitions presented by the authoritative sources quoted above, engineering invokes a wide range of activities productively utilizing the various applicable sciences. For simplicity, one can consider an engineering education as essentially developing a "box of necessary tools" to enable exploration and utilization of the mysteries of the physical and functional world around you.

The tools in that box will comprise a host of new nomenclatures, theorems, definitions, abstract mathematics, formulae, graphics, and experimentation to enable you to understand and create useful applications. It requires you to learn and master new "languages" that you will need to capture the explanation of processes, characteristics, and properties of matter and of nature. You will adopt and adapt portions of foreign languages that have developed over centuries of human experiences. This is particularly true of measures, standards, and universally observed natural phenomena; think Metric vs. English systems, as a beginning. The broad spectrum of engineering practices embrace an extensive range of very different phenomena, utilizing comprehension, understanding, and application to diverse ends. Thus, typically in practice, education and applied engineering focus narrowly on a defined specialty. There are numerous specialties that constitute a unique degree, as discussed in Chapter 4. This compares with the similar span of potential specialties in the Medical professions. In this comparison, the award of MD (Medical Doctor) is a broad designation that embraces a host of dedicated specialties within the scope of Medical Doctor. It expressly connotes the difference between MD and PhD (Doctor of Philosophy). Similarly, the engineering degrees usually carry a specialty designation, such as BSME (Bachelor of Science, Mechanical Engineering), BSISE (Bachelor of Science, Industrial & Systems Engineering), BSCE (Bachelor of Science, Civil Engineering). Some colleges prefer to simply cite BSE (Bachelor of Science, Engineering). Even so, a specialty has been featured in the education of such an awardee.

More to the point, the practice of engineering applies the basic natural sciences to the resolution of specific problems or creation of specific products. A comprehensive review of the fields of science is far beyond the scope of this book. A thorough topical overview is available from Wikipedia, entitled. "Outline of Science". The Wikipedia website also provides an excellent comparison of applied sciences versus basic sciences, as follows:

> *"Applied science focuses on the development of technology and techniques. In contrast, basic science develops scientific knowledge and predictions, principally in natural sciences but*

also in other empirical sciences, which are used as the scientific foundation for applied science. Basic science develops and establishes information to predict phenomena and perhaps to understand nature, whereas <u>applied science</u> uses portions of basic science to develop interventions via technology or technique to alter events or outcomes. Applied and basic sciences can interface closely in <u>research and development</u>. The interface between basic research and applied research has been studied by the National Science Foundation."

There are a number of people who identify as "Engineers" who base their claims on prior experiences in the military or in apprenticeships, deriving their "qualifications" from their use of manuals and or handbooks that provide techniques or formulae for computing "safe" stress levels for specific applications. Beware blindly accepting such "safe" limits for stresses and configurations since they are based upon "safety factors" which are actually *"Ignorance Factors".*

Why Ignorance Factors? Simple! Construction materials typically are marketed with an advertised range of both stress limits and deflections limits. To avoid actual physical testing of the materials to be used in a specific application, handbooks often provide increased dimensions, and calculate based on the minimum guaranteed material strength to avoid any possible over-stress of materials or components. Doing so denies adequate and proper sizing of components, increasing weight, cost, or even possibility of application.

Professional societies promote and support continuing education as a means of ensuring the continuing competence of certified and licensed engineers, and of preventing fraudulent use of the titles, "Engineer" or "Engineering". Pirating the title of engineer or claims of engineering are both immoral and illegal, since those titles are reserved for properly educated, certified and licensed practitioners. Professional Societies are also a valuable forum for informing practitioners of changes in laws, development of new or altered materials, processes, applications, tools, computer systems, and many other developments. They also provide a means of exchange of experiences and of observations of natural and people-driven changes in nature, such as "Global Warming" and resource exhaustion.

Another major function of professional societies is to promulgate policy changes dictated by courts or legislatures, and by state legislatures' adoptions of new or revised standards and practices. Since most states require formal licensing of practitioners, and continuing education is an inherent requirement for state licensure, Professional Societies provide a guide to seminars and symposia that provide acceptable credit hours of continuing education.

In recent years, mounting environmental concerns have given rise to a new concentration on the technical aspects of the recognition and mitigation of human contributions to such issues as atmospheric pollution, global warming and sea rise. Consequently, an entirely new engineering specialty has emerged. Environmental Engineering addresses the cause and effects of observed phenomena, and develops controls, reductions and avoidance measures.

CHAPTER 3

Motivation

If you are reading this book, you obviously have developed an interest in exploring whether Engineering is an appropriate career for you. This chapter in your exploration examines what has attracted you to seriously consider engineering as your career objective. Prospective engineering students usually have felt a strong attraction to such a demanding path to a life's work...far beyond simple curiosity. Perhaps someone in your family or a neighbor has given you some insights or cited experiences with engineering or with engineers. More likely, you have been impressed by engineers' accomplishments or personalities that were spectacularly portrayed in books, news, or movies.

My belief is simpler. Your primary motivation is most probably your own personal wonder about the <u>WHY</u> and the <u>HOW</u> of things and/or events that you have encountered. In my personal experience it was wanting to know exactly why every impressive thing I saw or experienced behaved as it did, and how it did so. As a child and continuing as a teen-ager, I always felt a compulsion to understand the why and the how. I strongly believe that those two mental questions fuel the curiosity that can only be satisfied through education and experience that clearly answers the why and how of a puzzle. In fact, I believe that if those two mental questions don't haunt you upon seeing a new challenge, you are not truly a "natural" for engineering. If you are blasé as to why or how, then engineering will likely prove to be more of a chore for you than a delight. As evidence, I refer you to a recent book that detailed the accomplishments of the Wright Brothers; the "fathers of heavier than air flight". They were two bicycle mechanics who, without any formal training or even apprenticeships, solved the secrets of heavier than air flight. They did so through dedicated observation of flights by birds, followed by thorough analyses of the characteristics they observed. By discerning and mimicking those flight characteristics of birds, and by using clever model gliders emulating a bird in flight they discovered both lift and control techniques. Thus they satisfied the very basic how and the why of heavier than air flight! Their trial and error "analysis" actually left moot the full answers, but their accomplishments actually encouraged continued study by others that led to the current degree of understanding and utilization of Aeronautical Engineering.

There is a set of personal attributes that suggest your suitability for an engineering education and career:

- Are you comfortable with math? Do you enjoy solving math problems or do you consider it an obstacle to dispense with as quickly as possible?
- Have you had basic Physics instruction? How about "Introductory Science"?
- Are you an organized person, or a bit sloppy in planning and performance to schedule?
- Are you inclined to precision in speech and thinking?
- Do you have patience in solving problems and situations, or is "good enough" your usual response?
- Do you have an appetite for detail and a memory to recall accepted facts?
- Do you usually recognize the difference between fact and opinion?
- Is your temperament tolerant of criticism?
- Have you acquired the necessary prerequisites to qualify for admission to the college you wish to attend? Such requirements are usually contained in the admission application.

Your honest response to the questions posed above will guide you to weigh your personal characteristics and inclinations against the challenges you may expect in an engineering education and career. Yes, you need to be a thinker and a determined student to fully grasp and understand the myriad natural laws, theories, analytical techniques and resources you will encounter. Engineering is a never-ending pursuit of knowledge, fueled by your basic education and enriched by your experiences in a lifetime career. It is a daily challenge and opportunity that is intellectually rewarding and soul satisfying.

Do not be discouraged by your high school ranking! Remember, you have been participating in a pseudo competition that is nowhere near even or equal. Your contemporaries may be enrolled in vastly different curricular programs; some much easier, others more difficult than yours. In the end comparison, there is no equivalency or adjustments to compensate for different degrees of challenge and difficulty. Ranking is just a scale of grade points in which easier courses provide higher scores. Extra-curricular activities enjoy significant value to those reviewing college/university applications.

Summary: As you consider your answers to the listed attributes, do not be put off by your response to any of them, but consider your response to the mix. Take the challenges with eyes wide open and understand that your success demands attention, resolve, and dedication. Do not expect your student life to be "One Big Party Time", as often depicted in the movies. The teaching flows constantly, quickly, and progressively, without allowed catch-up time. To fall behind is a short cut to failure. If you stumble, seek help without delay.

Still interested and determined? Go for it… and don't be discouraged from following your dream!

The Wright Brothers" by David McCullough; Simon & Shuster, 2015

CHAPTER 4

Fields of Engineering

By definition, "Engineering" is a term descriptive of a very wide range of specific fields of study and applications. While the basic "tools", the sciences, are all involved in all or most of them, there are many specific fields of specialization that involve unique sciences and study. Thus, curricula are developed supporting concentration in those unique fields of engineering and the award of degrees of specialization. Among those are:

- Aeronautical Engineering
- Architectural Engineering
- Astronomical Engineering
- Biomedical Engineering
- Chemical Engineering
- Civil Engineering
- Computer Engineering
- Electrical Engineering
- Environmental Engineering
- Industrial Engineering
- Marine Engineering
- Mechanical Engineering
- Metallurgical Engineering
- Mining Engineering
- Nuclear Engineering

From this partial listing one can appreciate the wide diversity of fields of engineering and the obvious need for focus and specialization. While it is true that the basic sciences are utilized in most of these specialties, there are also certain other sciences that are unique or nearly so that are not utilized in every engineering specialty. The syllabus for each specialty is therefore constructed to concentrate primarily on those sciences and practices required to ensure competence in that particular field. Typically, the first two years of all of the engineering curricula are essentially devoted to mastery of the basic sciences and analytical mathematics. The third year is a mix of "service courses" that provide insight into other specialties along with those unique to the chosen specialty. The fourth year focuses strongly on the chosen specialty, with advanced and updated concentration on specific applications. Most of the Majors listed above require extensive laboratory sessions (Labs) that provide hands-on demonstrations and experiences with practical applications of theoretical teachings. Labs typically require 2 to 3 hours each and yield low credit hours but provide invaluable experiences.

Moreover, the educational curricula developed for each career objective ensures mastery of all of the basic sciences that are necessary for the depth of understanding, scope and competence one seeks. Thus, certification of the understanding and subsequent mastery are progressively developed and ensured in ascending order by graduate Degrees in increasingly advanced and complex steps as follows:

- Engineering Technology (2 year training)
- Bachelor's Degree (BS or equal) (4 t0 6 years training)
- Master's Degree (MS or equal) (1 to 3 years training post BS)
- Doctor of Philosophy (PHD or equal) Depends upon program (2 to 4 years training post MS)

CHAPTER 5

Financial & Moral Support

Here we take a look at two very important aspects of your college career, financial and moral support. It is difficult to define exactly which of these two criteria is the most important. Without either of these, your performance will be heavily impacted. Any continuous struggle to finance your college education can place a heavy burden on your emotional and practical capabilities and on your concentration on your studies.

Without adequate financial support, there can seldom be college success. Fortunately, there are many sources available to the applicant, even without family funding.

- The educational benefits provided to military service veterans; formerly the G.I. Bill
- Academic Scholarships
- Athletic Scholarships *
- U.S. Government Academies; USMA, USNA, USAFA, USCGA
- Scholarships donated by alumni
- Competitive Scholarships awarded by organizations
- Federal Educational loans
- Federal Pell grants
- Conventional Bank Loans
- Personal Loans from Relatives

- Cooperative Employment offered by select Businesses (Alternate semesters for school and On-the job training)

Another means of minimizing college cost can be to begin your college program with enrollment in a local community college that has an agreement with your desired baccalaureate college for a transfer with its acceptance of full credit for your first two years' work. This arrangement can provide significant cost reductions through stay-home residence and continued family support. That may be further enhanced by your freedom to seek part-time employment.

Moral support is equally important. Undertaking and completing a full college program is a major commitment of time, energy, money, and self-evaluation. Any results other than success and a degree or degrees is a blow to your ego and an unrewarding experience. It is very helpful to have a family showing both interest and confidence in your progress at college. Recognition of the challenges you face to stay abreast of everything being fed to you at an amazing rate of speed helps to energize your daily grind. It will prove to be far removed from the fun-filled goof-off role depicted in Hollywood's party-land movies. You may find a surprising attitude among the cadre of instructors and professors you encounter. Many of them have no interest in documenting your attendance. They opine that you are paying for their instruction and therefore if, for whatever reason, you elect to skip a class or exercise, that is your loss, not theirs.

Without moral support from family and close friends, academic demands can become an intensive and heavy burden. You may feel a constant atmosphere of pressure to excel and to avoid any disappointment to yourself and family. The daily progressive presentations of new materials and assignments can seem to be unending, and your long-term goals can feel distant and without relief or reward in sight. Remember, your classmates are under the same pressures and are subject to the same strains you may be feeling at times. Forming close friendships with classmates can provide considerable stress-relief simply by sharing worries and concerns and hearing other ideas about coping with emerging issues. Remember the old saying, "misery loves company"? Gripe sessions between classmates often provide a way to lessen concerns.

> * _Caution_ - Athletic Scholarships can involve extensive commitments of time and consequent interference with academic schedules. I am not qualified to comment further on this form of scholarship. My personal experience with commitment to an athletic program was limited to a walk-on non-scholarship freshman year baseball team. I found it to be a serious interference with both study time and my ROTC commitment to a full-time cadet corps. I suggest that you carefully consider the near-certain potential impact that an athletic scholarship could have on your academic performance and on other extra-curricular activities.

CHAPTER 6

Getting Started

Timing: Your search for the best college selection should begin in earnest in your junior year of high school. There are many considerations to be identified and evaluated. Your high school may offer counselors to assist in your decisions by providing objective evaluations of your academic records, offering standard student aptitude testing, and admission requirements information and the reputational ranking of the colleges you are inclined to consider. Do not delay these important steps. In today's world, admission to selective colleges is a competition for available spaces in every program. Every element of the application process is critical. No admission is assured by a high class ranking or GPA. The entire "big picture" of your activities and achievements, boosted by an impressive personal presentation, is necessary to secure a place in the most desired colleges. Assume nothing! Prepare a selling application, using every positive endorsement you can honestly present.

Once you are convinced that an engineering career is your ultimate goal, you should begin the process of deciding the best path you should take. The path means your choice between several possible means of earning a Bachelor of Science Engineering Degree. Among your possible choices are:

- A conventional enrollment in a select college with a "Declared Engineering Major".

- A cooperative enrollment in a select college that partners with an established industrial business, that alternates college sessions with periods of on-the-job training by that business. This is a merger of education and practical experience that extends your time commitment by 2 to 3 years. Among the benefits of this program are the income and experience earned while in the work phases, and the likelihood of permanent employment after graduation.
- Enrollment in a local or nearby community college that typically provides the first two years of basic courses and has an agreement with a college or colleges to transfer all or agreed acceptable credits to the college of your choice, for guaranteed satisfaction of your chosen degree requirements.
- Enrollment in a technical institute or preparatory college that transfers the same basic credits as the community college. In some cases, this offers a preparatory advantage to some applicants who, for whatever reason, graduated from high schools with little or no exposure to the basic sciences.

These are critical choices for which you must fully consider the many factors that will ultimately determine your choices. Whatever your selections, you must take a realistic and honest evaluation of many factors. Principal among these are:

- Your academic performance and standing.
- Your financial prospects; availability of scholarships and/or loans.
- The goals you seek in your selected colleges; your depth of knowledge of the colleges you have considered; and your order of preference of your identified colleges.
- Your intensity of commitment to performance versus social activities and/or employment.
- Availability of financial and moral support from family and/ or employers.

- Travel and distance issues and expenses for visits to home and/or vacations.

Responding to the foregoing list of factors to consider is the beginning of your "Moments of Truth". This is the time to be brutally honest with yourself and to fully evaluate your responses. It is also a time to gather as much verified information as possible about each alternative to avoid unhappy realizations down-stream. So, let's take a look at how you need to think through each:

Academic Performance: Your record of academic performance begins with the formal Reports you have amassed through high school. That is a record you must evaluate with considerations of the relative challenges it imposed. For instance, a College Preparatory curricula far outweighs one of General Education, Shop, Automotive or Home Economics. Class standing can be deceptive since it is a simple comparison of accumulated grade scores, from highest to lowest, without consideration of the relative complexity of the undertakings. Looking ahead to college performance, measure your commitment to academic requirements versus your desire for social activities, recreational or sports participation, etc. Academics must take precedence, with other activities sharing what free time is left. For many, the choice is difficult since college time is considered to be a maturing process and priorities are competitive.

Financial Ability: This is a complex issue because it involves a lot of variables over which you may not have any control. It usually begins with the family ability to finance your education throughout the entire course to graduation. If this is not a problem, the other possibilities just become optional. If funding is not assured, then several other considerations can be considered. Next in preference are scholarships. Absent a full-ride athletic or academic scholarship, you may be eligible for partial scholarships awarded by various groups or sponsors. If scholarships are not available, there are educational loans available through various sources, with the Federal government ones being the most common. The most difficult means involves your employment while taking college courses. This is a path not to be taken lightly. It usually delays the traditional full-time commitment to college, and places a severe strain on your energy, stamina and waking time. Whichever path you take, the question of financing your education should be addressed and resolved. If you will need to have part-time employment to provide for living expenses, etc., this is the time to consider its availability and the effect it may have on your academic performance, and to adjust your goals accordingly.

Criteria: In selecting the most suitable college for you, there are many features and characteristics of the several colleges you are considering that should be fully explored and understood. Many will be patently undesirable because of their central focus. Obvious examples are the several Service Academies, such as West Point, The US Naval Academy, etc. Some others are specifically Liberal Arts centric, while some notably focus on research.

The internet is an incredible resource, whereby you can research every college that you wish to consider. Current information is posted there and you begin by simply searching for each selected college course catalog. That will lead you to a comprehensive set of details of specific degree programs, the course content of each. Additionally, there are other discussions such as a mission statement that describes the goals of the college; the requirements for entry and progress; and a host of other offerings. You will find the application forms and statement of supporting documents required and the schedules for submittal.

Your task is to first recognize exactly what you want in addition to the engineering education. If you have significant interest in social or religious co-education, then you will find that certain colleges best support those desires. If you are deeply interested in participating in sports, theatrics, languages, or other elective interests such as ROTC, they also must be honestly weighed in your decision. This is particularly true if you are seeking a related scholarship that funds your education.

After you decide to commit to engineering, your most important chores are to evaluate the colleges that offer the best combinations of your wants and needs. You then should acquire admission requirements and applications from each. Many of those you have selected will require you to present a personal letter of introduction when you submit your admission request. You may also need to obtain letters of recommendation from several unbiased, knowledgeable people. Based on what you have discovered, you can now make an informed selection and decide your order of preference. Next, you should collect all required data and records required by each and submit. Among those data usually required will be a certified transcript of your high school courses and grades. Use extreme caution to ensure total compliance with data and personal document requirements. Be aware that entry into most colleges is very competitive. Your careful response to stated requirements is a major factor in that competition

While you await responses from the colleges to which you have applied, you should begin to identify and gather all of your basic necessities, and accessories you will take with you. In your acceptance letter, you may find suggestions for optional needs and a list of required clothing, equipment, documents, and records you must bring with you at registration.

You may have the option to decide whether you would plan to live on-campus or off-campus in the local community. If you select on-campus housing, you may also have the privilege of selecting a roommate or having that assignment made by the college. This is an important choice because the relationship between roommates can be either supportive or disruptive. If the choice is made by the college, you or your roommate may find it less than desirable. Just be aware that you have recourse should the situation become problematic. If you choose off-campus housing, you need to explore the available-housing market. College towns usually have a listing of apartments, or other facilities for rent and support. As a final step, it may be wise to schedule a personal visit to the campus and the nearby communities. Most colleges offer a visitation program that features guided tours of the campus and of the various academic programs and extra-curricular activities.

PART TWO
AT COLLEGE

CHAPTER 7

Schedules and Assignments

Your application for enrollment identified your objective course of study and on that basis your admission will have generated your specific assignments to the first-semester classes that will have been scheduled for you at your initial registration. Registration is your formal matriculation when you arrive on campus.

From your college catalog, and possibly by information accompanying your acceptance letter, you can see the courses assigned for your first semester. At your initial check-in and registration, you will be welcomed and given your basic college orientation and class schedule along with other documents that provide details for your life on campus. After this initial semester, you may have the opportunity to select the schedules for following semesters and course requirements, based on the availability of appropriate classes. This procedure may vary between colleges, but the intent is to ensure orderly completion of requirements in the order most beneficial to you. You will also be given instruction as to required books, report forms, computers, printers, etc. and information as to on-campus services. If you have selected on-campus living, you may also be given a dormitory assignment.

In the first meeting of each of your assigned classes, you will be introduced to the subject matter to be covered, provided the objectives of the course, given details of any specific supplies, texts, and required reading, and attendance rules. Some instructors are quite adamant about attendance; others do not insist on rigorous attendance or even bother to record presence or absence. Some simply acknowledge your adult right to choose, noting the only loser when lack of attendance results in missed materials are those who elected to skip the class! Be aware that this choice should not be abused and is almost certain to result in your diminished understanding.

Be aware that colleges do not offer every course every semester. If, for whatever reason, you need to schedule a specific course that is not a current semester requirement, it may not be available when you need it. This situation can arise when you must miss or drop a course in its normal scheduled semester or period due to schedule conflict, illness, accident, or failure of first attempt. Avoid this potential disruption if at all possible!

CHAPTER **8**

Your Load Bearing Capacity

There is an old saying, "Don't bite off more than you can chew!" That is good advice as you embark on a challenging course of study. Engineering is no pushover! It very well may require your complete attention as you progress through the program. You are going to be tempted by a number of interesting and desirable optional activities. A well-rounded education and satisfying college experience provides opportunities for character growth beyond technical competence. There are social, religious, regional, academic fraternal, trade, musical, intramural, sports, language, and a host of other optional activities that may appeal to you. Just keep in mind that each such extra-curricular activity demands time and devotion that competes for your time against your academic demands. Your choices of the extras should be thoughtfully balanced against commitments demanded by your academic program requirements.

If you are contemplating taking either a part-time job or pursuing a degree through evening classes, to offset college expenses, you will be signing-in to a very high stress commitment that is fraught with conflict between the demands of each. In fact, it may be impossible for you to resolve successive schedule conflicts, particularly with mandatory laboratory sessions. Either way, combining school and work demands produces significant to overwhelming stress and is certain to impact your performance and morale. It most certainly will

31

impact or deny any other extra-curricular activities you might desire. If such an arrangement is necessary to finance your education, consider adopting reduced semester schedules over an extended period to spread your college courses over a longer span of years, or simply not taking any summer breaks. Be aware, however, there are certain programs that already require summer semesters so that option may not provide enough pressure relief to be a plausible option.

Recognizing the relatively fast-pace of college courses, compared to your experiences in high school, you should take a well-considered look at how much, and exactly what, you are willing to commit to, and what you honestly believe you can reasonably expect to be able to accomplish, in terms of quality and timeliness of performance. This is critical to both your success and to your health. Do not try to analyze this by yourself. This is what course advisors are for. Tap their experience and determine what is even acceptable in schedule arrangements, and what they can provide in creative suggestions.

Your review of load-bearing should also consider day-to-day disruptions and commitments to mundane daily or weekly tasks that demand your attention, time and expense. These vary according to the living arrangements you have made at enrollment. Specifically, if you have elected on-campus living with room, meals and laundry services provided, then such demands are not a significant issue except for the time devoted to taking advantage of them. If they are not provided, then you must arrange for each and devote time to their completion. Off-campus living demands considerable time to perform all of those and more. Another matter to consider is the travel between home and college for holidays, breaks and celebrations. All such issues cause stress and planning. These matters also require you to take a good thoughtful look and factoring into your conclusions. As you can readily see, this is a formidable task, best not left to chance.

Finally, if you are finding the materials being presented to be difficult and demanding inordinate amounts of time or, worse yet, difficult to absorb or understand, *get help!* Do not let foolish pride interfere with seeking assistance. Help is available for the asking. Fellow students are always there to help and your instructor's help can also be had. Remember, if <u>you</u> fail, <u>your instructors have also failed</u>. Do not fall behind…<u>get help!</u>

CHAPTER 9

Critique and Confirmation of Major

Once you are settled in at the college of your choice, and have completed your first year of study, you will have developed a reaction to the demands, the quality, and the rate of instruction you have received. It will be natural for you to have strong impressions concerning the pressure you felt and the satisfaction or lack thereof that you feel about your experiences.

In all probability, you will have noted a significant increase in the demands placed on you for effort and concentration. As earlier noted, the rate of instruction is much higher than you had been used to in high school. The expectations of the instructors in high school were tempered by averaging the collective capabilities of the students (a cohort). You are now part of a new cohort, wherein expectations are considerably greater because of your admittance to college was predicated upon a new and higher cohort average. A paraphrased but beautiful, quotation from the Holy Bible, Luke, 12:48, *"from whom to which much was given, much is expected"* explains the expected higher average.

You may also experience, what appears to be an unnecessary repetition of materials you actually covered in high school, particularly in mathematics, chemistry and physics. That is to be expected and should not lead to your mistaken impression that the later courses will be equally familiar. Some first year, seemingly repetitive courses, are simply accommodating the likely differences between various high schools and their scope of coverage. It is a means of levelling the preparation of the class as a whole for what follows. You will soon be challenged by the successive courses to follow. Do not expect the later materials to be equally familiar or easy! If you are finding the materials being presented to be difficult or demanding inordinate amounts of time, or worse yet, difficult to absorb or understand, *get help!* Do not let foolish pride interfere with seeking assistance.

As you progress through your academic years, it is a good practice to review your status against the full program plan that is defined in your current course catalog. You will have a full syllabus of what is to follow in your course catalog, so there should be no surprise as to the required courses leading to your desired degree. Are you still content with the path you have selected and the degree program you have selected? Have you considered the electives available to supplement the required courses of your program? Available electives are also clearly shown in that catalog. and other options that allow you to select courses of interest that are not necessarily associated with your selected major. If you are having second thoughts about your chosen degree program, this is the time for a discussion with your course advisors to ascertain whether you should make a change in degree objectives. If you have strong reservations about committing to the established path to your degree, this may be the time to investigate alternatives. From my personal perspective, that is exactly what I found as I prepared to enter my senior year. The senior syllabus required selection between four concentration paths in Mechanical Engineering. I determined that none of the four was what I wanted to focus on in my future career. I wanted more flexibility and further concentrations on applications of the basic sciences and arts of engineering. I found my goals in Industrial and Systems Engineering and, with cooperation by the two department heads, arranged my transfer to that college. Such a late transfer put me in a bind for time to catch up necessary credit hours and to schedule required courses. Despite accepting course credit hour overloads in remaining quarters (VPI was then on quarters vs semesters) and two summer quarters, I couldn't manage to complete all requirements in time for graduation with my class. That took one more quarter after completing my prior ROTC commitment to two years of active duty. Thus, a lesson in failing to look forward early enough to avoid such a penalty in time. Actually, it resulted in a bonus, however, in that I did receive considerably more insight into applied mechanical engineering courses than straight industrial and systems engineering curricula provided. On balance, a good deal!

As my experience illustrates, beware of waiting too long to undertake a thoughtful review of your personal goals and interests. Time, maturation and other circumstances may alter your insight and goals

CHAPTER **10**

Parallel Objectives; Personal Satisfaction

In Chapter 8, I warned against undertaking too many extra-curricular activities. There is another choice you could have made or considered that entails even more stress and demand on your time and energy; the decision to pursue dual majors. That decision should not be made lightly. Be certain to fully research and carefully evaluate the additional workload that would be required to satisfy the requirements of both.

The more common parallel objectives are:

- Full or part-time employment while pursuing your degree.
- Athletic scholarships requiring adherence to rigorous schedules and off-campus travel.
- Selecting electives that support a desired future employment, such as a foreign language to enhance qualification for foreign-based occupations.
- Enrollment in Reserve Officer Training (ROTC) to earn a military commission; especially in a full-time cadet corps program.
- Participation in a demanding music program such as a student band, choral group, stage performances, etc.
- Overseas semesters in student exchange programs.

Each of the above choices place major demands on your time, your concentration, and your energies. Chapter 8 suggests your careful analysis of your load-bearing capacity. The additional demands associated with your commitment to any of them is tantamount to voluntarily increasing your obligations and surrendering your otherwise free time. The commitments are both direct and indirect. Before you decide to engage in any such objectives, be aware of the reduced uncommitted time left to you for unplanned but desirable choices for activities, events, travel, etc.

Chapter 9 suggests that you periodically evaluate the impact of your choices of major and extra-curricular activities have upon your performance and satisfaction. Only you have the advantage of recognizing the effects of any over-reaching. Your college experience should not be overly stressful nor a constant feeling of grasping nor of desperation. Rather, it should be rewarding in the sense of progressive satisfaction of your desire to understand former mysteries and an appetite for further disclosures. If you are feeling lost or falling behind in what the courses are teaching, it may be time to reevaluate any participation you may have made in any electives, and increase the available time and energy to rectify the cause of your discontent.

It may also be the time to reconsider the original goals you earlier set in the light of your personal satisfaction with what you now see as your potential career opportunities. Consider whether the chosen concentration or subsequent employment in that concentration is likely to satisfy your desires for a career. Decide whether you should consider alternatives more closely aligned with what you now recognize as your developing career interests?

By no means should your college experience be a drudgery, with total dedication to a narrow course of study with no time allowed for you to mature in a well-balanced program that permits and encourages your participation in far more than purely academic interests. Your college years should support your development from shallow youth to accomplished and inquisitive adulthood. It should be a memorable and treasured set of experiences with expanded interests in a wide variety of activities. You will be exposed to situations, personalities, and perspectives that may be foreign to you but are part of a well-developed culture in another region or country. It is also a time to appreciate the scope of new and extraordinary philosophies that challenge your concepts of ethics, government, law, customs, travel, languages, and social norms. You will find that your instructors, professors, and college operating staff are a generally diverse group; some with distinct quirks that provide interesting experience-driven perspectives on a wide variety of subjects...some related to your course materials and others that are purely personal rants. Keep an open mind, but pay close attention to whether such "observations" are reasonable to you or are so unusual as to be even comical or ridiculous.

As you progress, your personal satisfaction with your complete experiences will be determined by a balanced participation in a variety of activities beyond the strictly academic portion of your college days. College is also a social journey, introducing you to a host of unique personalities in both fellow students and in the wide range of instructors and professors. In most colleges, you will encounter students from all parts of the USA, and from a variety of foreign countries. The age groups will vary widely as well as the depth of experiences of students and staff. If you elect ROTC as a parallel course, you will meet veteran active duty officers and NCOs who offer unique perspectives on a military career. They also present a real-world view on sensitive subjects that impact a military career, from government to politics.

CHAPTER 11

Dealing with Adversity and Interferences

It is not unusual for circumstances and problems to arise in the course of a college education. Many factors can impact or halt an orderly progress from start to finish of a nominal four year program intended to lead to satisfactory completion and graduation with a desired engineering degree. Many of such issues can result from events beyond the control or influence of the student. Others are the consequence of choices or poor performances. Here are just some of the causes that may arise:

- Scheduling problems
- Financial problems
- Illness & consequent delays in completing required courses
- Family problems
- Injury & lost attendance
- Unavailability of required courses
- Transfer from original program selection to new Department
- Required repeat of required course(s)
- Military service
- Vacation or travel

Each of the foregoing can have the unhappy consequence of requiring unusual means of corrections to regain schedule, or to cause unrecoverable loss of sequence and timely completion of all degree requirements. Each issue requires a closely tailored method of recovery or the extension of completion dates. Once the planned sequencing of required courses is disrupted, a new set of problems can surface and create further delays. Primarily, these are the unavailability of out-of-sequence individual courses that are mandatory for satisfactory completion. Sometimes such irregularities can be resolved through negotiated substitution of available courses that are deemed by the college to be an acceptable alternate. Usually, such issues are only resolved through careful schedule manipulation to permit scheduling when the course is available, often creating an overload of credit hours in a given semester, or by recovering during an otherwise unnecessary summer semester.

Often, because of the direct cause, the emerging problems are unexpected and sudden, and unknown until they occur. In such cases, one must determine the probable impact of the interruption and, in concert with the college, ascertain whether the interruption can be recovered, or simply accept the loss of time and credit. That will be determined by how far along in the courses one is when the interruption strikes. Often, the resolution is to "bite the bullet" and simply reschedule the remainder of the program. In the first years, summer semesters can often be used to regain schedule.

As an example of a sudden and unavoidable occurrence in my freshman year, I had a personal experience when my father fell ill with what was diagnosed as terminal. It was very close to the year's end and examinations. I was quickly approved for an emergency leave with deferred examinations until a summer break make-up. Fortunately, Dad staged a remarkable recovery and I was able to complete the exams during the summer without interfering with a normal start of my sophomore year. Whatever any emerging problem might be, it is essential that you inform appropriate college staff and seek assessment of the likely impact on current work and orderly schedules. Together, you and the college can develop a suitable program to minimize the interruption and afford a timely and affordable resolution.

PART THREE
POST-COLLEGE CAREERS

CHAPTER 12

Preparing for Employment

As you enter your senior year and look forward to graduation and the search for the ideal job in your chosen field, there are several tasks to complete. First on your list should be to review the various areas of employment that most appeal to you. That should have been on your mind and possibly have influenced your declared major, and your choice of concentrations for your senior year. That might have been categorical rather than any consideration of the industries or businesses you would like to join. Depending upon how intensive your evaluations might have been as discussed in chapter 9, you may now be making your first singling-out of exactly what field of endeavor you want to enter.

Having made your selection or selections, your next chore is to evaluate the opportunities that may be open to you in that field. This is a critical step that requires your objective investigation of a wide range of the employers' functions that create their needs for new graduates. Among these are:

- Private business or Government positions
- Current and projected states of the national economy
- Present & projected specialties reflected in published business and political analyses
- If inclined to the business sector, what is the nature of your choice, e.g., Research, Manufacture, Sales, Operations, Services, Education, etc.

- Most desirable corporation or company reputation and market strength
- Geographic locations

Be honest in your evaluation of potential locations with due consideration of location of your target employers. Think of what effects your selected employment's location may have on your social and entertainment preferences, the travel involved in maintaining close contact with friends, family, holiday celebrations, church, and various club memberships. Complete relocations can be extremely disruptive and expensive, and produce very uncomfortable and lonely off-duty periods.

In good economic times, certain entry-level engineering skills are in high demand and can be in very attractive locations. Others can be in remote or even foreign locations. Your consideration of target employers should fully anticipate the impact such locations will likely have on your satisfaction. As time passes, you may marry and begin a family. Then, your location may present a major problem since new issues will arise when two or even more personalities and preferences enter the equation.

Some possible employment locations hold unique social, cultural and historical characteristics that may be foreign to you and that tend to isolate or label "outsiders". Think "Big City" or "Small Town" locations that may be quite different to you; or locations that are heavily focused on a single industry, farming, or collegiate concentration. Language and dialect can also create personal comfort issues. Those considerations are more germane to foreign countries where your language is the foreign one. Other major attributes to be investigated are the cost-of-living index and any ecological constraints that impact comfortable living, such as water use limitations, etc. These are mentioned simply to awaken you to factors that may not be obvious at first glance but form a significant potential impact on your overall satisfaction.

CHAPTER 13

Job Hunting and Interviewing

Once you have determined the specific field and several potential employers that seem to fit your goals and interests, you need to connect with your college advisors and whichever department schedules on-campus interviews, and make arrangements for a person to person interview. Many colleges have a well-organized program that arranges for on-campus interviews by a variety of potential employers that seek first-selection opportunities. Typically, they schedule interested students to meet with visiting recruiters that have requested the opportunity to meet with interested students on a given date. Based upon those interviews, recruiters may then invite selected interviewees for a company visit for further mutual evaluation and to decide whether to offer employment.

If your college does not host on-campus interviews, then you must independently research the employers in which you are interested and determine how best to make a direct personal inquiry seeking their current employment opportunities. Your inquiry should clearly establish your genuine interest in employment and perhaps explain why you have such an interest in the company. Finally, you may request available company information together with an employment application.

Whichever of the foregoing introductions to prospective employers you follow, successful contact will likely require your preparation of an introductory expression of interest and request for an interview. That is your first opportunity to make a positive impression on a personal interviewer. Remember, you are selling a product... YOU! Much of the information you will provide is in your completion of a standard applications form provided by the company. In the narrative segment, you will have the opportunity to impress management by demonstrating that you have researched the company to familiarize yourself with the company and have a genuine interest in becoming a part of its team.

In your responses, be humble in the sense that you realize you have much to learn and an eagerness to accept a learning position. Demonstrate that you have the education, attitude and ambition to grow into a valuable employee. Online and from your local libraries, there are many guides available to you to properly prepare for the interview and for your initial information exchanges with their representative. Be prepared for the interview, and do not hesitate to request any and all information you need to evaluate not only the business opportunity itself, but also the whole picture of being an employee of their company in the location or locations involved. One word to the wise is to determine the typical career course an engineer employee follows. Is the work limited to a single location only or would there typically be a chain of transfers with development and expansion of your qualifications that offer advancement but require relocations? Determine whether there is a typical path for advancement?

Once you have completed your interviews and await an expected offer of employment, consider the peripheral aspects of such employment. Does acceptance mean a physical relocation? If so, does the proposed location appeal to you and family? How does the cost-of-living index at the offered location compare to your present location? Is the cost of such a physical relocation borne by or shared with the employer? Will the position offered involve frequent business travel?

If so, are the travel costs borne entirely by the employer? Are there company-paid or discounted benefits such as health insurance, life insurance, specialty training, paid vacation, continuing education, tools and equipment, etc.? From the sum of the answers to the foregoing, consider the financial pros and cons of the offered employment

Finally, understand that your employment will be an investment by your employer with scant return until you develop and apply necessary skills and experience. Be patient and receptive to critique.

CHAPTER 14

Professional Certification & Licensure

Professional certification is a licensure process imposed by individual states that provides a documented assurance by the state's designated and authorized agency of the qualifications demonstrated by the licensee to practice a specific profession within that issuing state. It sets forth a formal schedule of licensure, usually annually, for confirmation of compliance with continuing education requirements, evidenced by a renewed license that must be displayed as appropriate, and cited as required, on specified documentation associated with any specific project. Typically, that requirement is satisfied by stamp or impression of the identity and license number of the certifying engineer.

Many states offer and provide the practice of Reciprocity, wherein qualification and licensure by one state is recognized and accepted by another as full compliance with its own requirements.

Practices of licensure vary widely between states and often impose additional requirements not imposed by other states. One such requirement is the specific capability to address the unique effects of earthquakes.

The procedure to earn a certification and license to practice usually involves a two-phase examination, comprising an "Engineer-in-training" examination and another more intensive demonstration of competence in applying engineering judgement and understanding through a second examination. That final examination follows a specified period of working under the supervision of a certified engineer. Another variance is the required accumulated time in acceptable applied experience before one is permitted to undertake the first phase of a two-phase testing sequence. In other states, one may apply for and undertake the first phase examination immediately upon graduation or even in the final semester leading to graduation. The exact requirements of the state in which you intend to practice should be explored as soon as you develop an interest in certification for any future plans.

The National Society of Professional Engineers (NSPE) is a professional organization that was formed to represent the duly registered and licensed professional engineers across the country. As representatives and a voice for the profession, it establishes and defines acceptable practices and limitations that are widely accepted as the standards for professional engineers. A major function of the society is to protect the profession against intrusion, manipulation, usurpation, and imitation. The NSPE monitors state laws and proposed changes and offers commentary to illuminate the impacts and effects of any such changes on both engineers and their clients and employers. It also lobbies state and federal agencies and membership to adopt policies protective of public safety and recognition of impending threats. Finally, NSPE has adopted and promulgated a Canon of Ethics to guide engineers' practices.

CHAPTER 15

Career Satisfaction

Beginning a new career is usually the beginning of an entirely new life style. Accordingly, there were, or will be, considerable adjustments to be made in your expectations, concerns, and your degree of satisfaction. After a long period of commitment to a structured environment and mandated series of objectives, you have found you are now in a new but similar situation of having to comply with a new employee's structured environment of assigned tasks and schedules. The difference now, however, is that you are the sole judge of how your progress meets your expectations and desires. This evaluation may be intentional or simply an internal reaction that manifests in contentment or in dissatisfaction. In either case, this is a natural process that everyone experiences at numerous and frequent times throughout their full career. While this can be an ongoing and unconscious assessment, it is important that you understand what triggers your feelings and not rush to judgement. Remember that you are making major adjustments to all aspects of your life, not just to your employment. Also recognize that many factors combine to form your total satisfaction or dissatisfaction. Consider which of those factors are temporary and/or transient, and which ones you can control. Realize also that the satisfaction of your immediate family (mate and children) is of prime importance. This is a time to be self-critical and completely honest. William Shakespeare wrote a magnificent admonition in his play, "Hamlet", Act 1, Scene III as follows:

"This above all, to thine own self be true, and it will follow, as the night the day, Thou canst not then be false to any man".

At the outset of a new employment, both employer and employee begin the process of evaluation of the "fit" of the employee, within the mutual expectations of performance, attitude, adaptability and personality. You will evaluate your impressions of the employer as an organization, as management, the morale of the employees and managers, and the complete environment within the organization as it affects you. During the initial phase of your new job, you will develop your own opinions of the policies, practices, attitudes, and motivations of both direct management and senior management. Those opinions will collectively influence or determine your satisfaction with your position and prospects for advancement. Be patient but not hesitant to correct a serious misgiving as to the potential for ultimate satisfaction.

It is understandable that your employer must develop an early assessment of your capabilities and potential fit within the organization. It is important that you recognize that your first few months are a mutual assessment period wherein your potential as a valuable employee is under scrutiny while you are simultaneously evaluating how well this job fits your desires and goals for the future. It is a courtship of sorts as both employer and employee take the measure of mutual satisfaction. Some employers actually employ a defined probation period after which permanency of employment is assured or terminated.

From your perspective, consider the prospects you see or infer from observation of co-workers, and from your own experiences. A long series of pure rote assignments may well indicate that your potential for future advancement is limited, or that opportunities for advancement are limited by other factors. Your personal periodic performance reviews provided by many employers may provide the clues you need for an accurate evaluation of your advancement potential. Large corporations with multiple locations may condition advancement opportunities to transfers to other locations. Except for new employees who were cooperative program (co-op) students and those having had between-semesters internships with appropriate companies, the average engineering graduate will present with little or no actual experience on which to base expectations of just what to expect of his first few months of employment. It would be a brand new experience during which his employer can gauge his aptitude for meaningful contribution to company objectives. It is also an initiation into the world of applied productive technical work.

It is not at all unusual for any new engineer to feel ill-used or even wasted by assignment to mundane and repetitive tasks. That is a period of acclimation for you, and probing by management to determine your ability to adapt to and master the methodology and processes your employer has developed to accomplish work. Be patient and absorb and understand the "why" behind that process. This is a learning process and should lead to increasingly complex and interesting further assignments. Your employer wants more from you even more rapidly than you do. You are, after all, an investment! The more you can do and the quicker you can do it well, the more valuable you are to him and the further and faster you will progress.

The real value of this periodic personal review of your satisfaction may come from a wider look at where you are relative to any goals you have established for yourself, and a thoughtful revisit to the interests that convinced you to accept this employment and your basic decision to undertake engineering in the first place. Ask yourself, is this what you really enjoy doing and will it lead to what you really still want to do? Recognize that a change in dreams is the product of daily living and maturing. You may also encounter life-changing experiences or exposure to previously unknown, emerging or new challenges in engineering or other fields. Examples of such recognitions are evolving computer systems, artificial intelligence, politics, law, and physics.

This entire chapter advocates for your periodic self-analyses of your degree of satisfaction with all aspects of your total life. That begins with your satisfaction with your full life in your present employment, including position, location, prospects for advancement, earnings, stability, demands and limitations on your free time, and family impacts. If that analysis reveals underlying dissatisfaction, explore what the contributing factors are and consider what changes need to be made to ensure significant improvements or corrections. If that indicates a need to seek new employment, initiate a careful and reliable review of possibilities and weigh each against your recognized needs, not just the potential employment but also to determine the other life-issues that should heavily influence any decision to make such a change.

Epilogue

My principal objective in writing this book was simply to provide a balanced look at the scope and career of "Engineering" through the eyes of a veteran practitioner. It is by no means a comprehensive analysis of the broad range of engineering careers available to you as a degreed engineer. Rather, It is a guide suggesting your thoughtful consideration of factors that may not be immediately obvious to anyone contemplating pursuit of the requisite education and the future impacts on career work, job locations, and life style.

There are certain work-related facts your experience will reveal that must be recognized and accommodated throughout a successful and satisfying engineering career:

1. In practice, nearly all design is a compromise of ideals. The many variables involved in creating a design require evaluations and selections that must be combined to develop a design that is both practical and satisfactory within the essential parameters that must be evaluated and implemented. Among these are:

    -   Specification requirements;
    -   Technical and performance requirements that are imposed by law or invoked in customer contract and purchase orders;

- Weight; Dimensions; Volume and space availability;
- Fabrication methodology;
- Tooling; Chemical & electrical stability & compatibility;
- Service life expectancy,
- Preservation,
- Access for maintenance & overhaul,
- Material & component availability;
- Cost;
- Material & Component procurement Lead time;
- Power requirements;
- Environmental impacts.

2. In science, there is a huge gap between fact and belief. Fact requires absolute and undeniable proof. Belief may be universal and, though seemingly convincing, remains incapable of absolute proof. Such beliefs are properly recognized as theories. Many such theories acquire such massive belief that they are actually but erroneously treated by many as fact. An example of such are the theories of primary causation in observed and predicted Global Warming and atmospheric quality. While many theories are treated as fact in designs, that can be a dangerous and costly assumption. Accordingly, application of such factors should be recognized as a prudent consideration, accepted as such by all involved parties.

3. There are many enigma that modern technology cannot yet explain. Among those are the methodology and equipage used in the construction of the Great Pyramids, the Roman Coliseum, and various temples and structures discovered in very remote South American and European locations. The largest challenging inexplicable puzzle is the Outer Space Universe and its seemingly infinite boundaries. The theories involved compose the ultimate conflict between belief and fact!

4. Science is a demanding task-master! Ultimately, it challenges the human mind to identify, recognize, understand, and properly accommodate all of the pertinent facts involved in every technical application. To consciously overlook any involved operative fact is not only dishonest but also a potentially fatal blunder.

5. As I was reminded by the FAA examiner who approved my pilot-qualification test flight, my earned Pilots License was simply a license to continue to learn through experience! Such is the actual meaning of your engineering degree. Continued learning is a non-stop lifetime requirement for engineers and for all other professionals.

CPSIA information can be obtained
at www.ICGtesting.com
Printed in the USA
BVHW081820200421
605388BV00006B/860